JUL   2013

Hamsters

and Other Pet Rodents

Editorial:
Editor in Chief: Paul A. Kobasa
Project Manager: Cassie Mayer
Writer: Natasha Anastasia Tarpley
Researcher: Cheryl Graham
Manager, Contracts & Compliance
  (Rights & Permissions): Loranne K. Shields
Indexer: David Pofelski

**Manufacturing/Production/
Graphics and Design:**
Director: Carma Fazio
Manufacturing Manager:
  Steven K. Hueppchen
Production/Technology Manager:
  Anne Fritzinger
Manager, Graphics and Design:
  Tom Evans
Coordinator, Design Development
  and Production:
  Brenda B. Tropinski
Senior Designer: Isaiah Sheppard
Photographs Editor: Kathy Creech
Cartographer: John Rejba

For information about other World Book publications, visit our website at http://www.worldbookonline.com or call 1-800-WORLDBK (967-5325).

For information about sales to schools and libraries, call 1-800-975-3250 (United States), or 1-800-837-5365 (Canada).

World Book, Inc.
233 N. Michigan Avenue
Chicago, IL 60601
U.S.A.

Library of Congress Cataloging-in-Publication Data
Hamsters and other pet rodents.
    p. cm. -- (World Book's animals of the world)
  Includes index.
  Summary: "An introduction to hamsters and other pet rodents, presented in a highly illustrated, question-and-answer format. Features include fun facts, glossary, resource list, index, and scientific classification list"-- Provided by publisher.
  ISBN 978-0-7166-1370-1
  1. Rodents as pets--Juvenile literature. 2. Hamsters as pets--Juvenile literature. I. World Book, Inc.
SF459.R63.H36 2010
636.935'6--dc22
                                    2009020165

World Book's Animals of the World
Set 6: ISBN: 978-0-7166-1365-7
Printed in China by Leo Paper Products LTD., Heshan, Guangdong
2nd printing August 2011

Picture Acknowledgments: Cover: © Juniors Bildarchiv/Alamy Images; © Jozsef Szasz-Fabian, Shutterstock; © Matt Staples, istockphoto; © WILDLIFE/Alamy Images; © Horst Klemm, Masterfile.

© C. Steimer, ARCO/age fotostock 31; © Arco Images/Alamy Images 51; © blickwinkel/Alamy Images 23; © Juniors Bildarchiv/Alamy Images 7, 13, 17, 21, 33, 41, 53; © Michael Krabs, imagebroker/Alamy Images 35; © Top-Pet-Pics/Alamy Images 29; © WILDLIFE/Alamy Images 5, 47; © Paul Bricknell, Dorling Kindersley 27, 55; © Steve Teague, Dorling Kindersley 25, 59; © Robert Manella, Iconica/Getty Images 15; © istockphoto 37, 39; © Janet Bailey, Masterfile 49; © Horst Klemm, Masterfile 43; © Shutterstock 3, 4, 19, 45, 57, 61.

Illustrations: WORLD BOOK illustration by Roberta Polfus 9.

World Book's Animals of the World

Hamsters
and Other Pet Rodents

WORLD
BOOK

a Scott Fetzer company
Chicago
www.worldbookonline.com

Contents

What Is a Hamster?

A hamster is a small, furry animal with bright eyes and a barrel-shaped body. Hamsters are mammals—animals that feed their young with milk made by the mother. They belong to a group of animals called rodents (gnawing mammals). Other rodents include mice, guinea pigs, and gerbils.

Hamsters are probably best known for their seemingly endless supply of energy. (Picture a hamster running on a wheel!) They are also known for their ability to store large amounts of food in pouches under their cheeks. When full, the pouches can make their cheeks puff out like a trumpet player blowing into his or her horn.

Hamsters can make great pets. Once they are comfortable in their new home, they enjoy attention and are curious about the world around them. Hamsters are also clean animals and are fairly easy to care for. But even so, it is important to take the right steps to help your pet stay healthy and happy.

A curious hamster

What Does a Hamster Look Like?

Hamsters often have adorable faces. They have large, bright eyes, whiskers, and a pouch under their cheeks for storing food and nesting material. The pouch is sort of like a pocket. It extends from the cheeks to the shoulders and is hardly noticeable unless it's very full.

Like all rodents, hamsters have two top and two bottom front teeth, which are called incisors *(ihn SY zuhrs)*. Incisors keep growing all the time.

Most hamsters have only a stub of a tail at the end of their stocky, tubelike bodies. The short tail sets the hamster apart from many other members of the rodent family, such as mice and rats, which have long tails.

Depending on the breed, a hamster's fur can come in a variety of lengths and textures: long or short, coarse or silky, puffy or sleek, straight or curly. A hamster's coat can also range in color from brown, black, and gray to white or red.

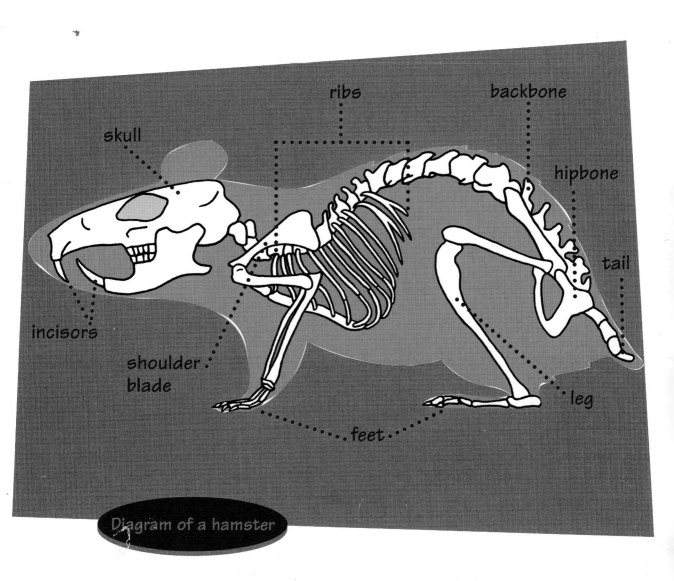

skull

ribs

backbone

hipbone

incisors

tail

shoulder
blade

leg

feet

Diagram of a hamster

9

Where Do Hamsters Live in the Wild?

Hamsters were once found in a variety of regions and climates. The hamster most likely to exist in the wild today is the common hamster. Larger than the average pet hamster, common hamsters have a raccoonlike coat of black and brown.

Common hamsters were once abundant throughout Central Asia and Central Europe. However, farmers have made an effort to eliminate the common hamster because it is known to raid crops grown on local farms for food. This has led to a severe decrease in the number of wild common hamsters.

Though not as plentiful, wild hamsters can also be found in East Asia and the Middle East.

Wild hamsters live in burrows that are like underground tunnels. When they are not traveling for miles in search of food, hamsters in the wild spend much of their time in their burrows, safe from extreme heat or cold and from other animals.

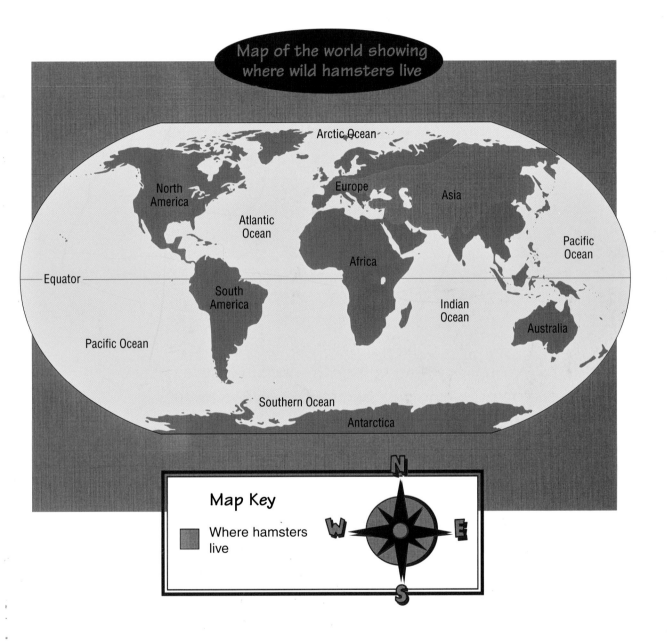

Map of the world showing where wild hamsters live

Arctic Ocean

North America

Europe

Asia

Atlantic Ocean

Pacific Ocean

Africa

Equator

South America

Indian Ocean

Pacific Ocean

Australia

Southern Ocean

Antarctica

Map Key

Where hamsters live

N
W   E
S

11

How Did Breeds of Hamsters Develop?

There are many different breeds of pet hamsters. A breed is a group of animals that have the same type of ancestors. Because of hamsters' popularity as a household pet, people began breeding them for certain desired physical traits, such as hair of a certain color, texture, or length.

There are several different species (kinds) of hamsters. One of the most popular pet hamster species is the golden, or Syrian, hamster. As its name implies, the golden hamster is usually gold with a white stomach. In the wild, golden hamsters lived in dry, rocky places, where this coloring helped the animal to blend in with its surroundings. People have bred the golden hamster to produce coats of a variety of colors, textures, and patterns.

Another common species is the dwarf hamster, which gets its name because of its small size. Members of the various dwarf species of hamsters have become widely available due to breeding.

Dwarf hamsters

13

How Big Do Hamsters Get? How Long Do They Live?

Golden hamsters typically grow to be between 6 and 8 inches (15.2 and 20.3 centimeters) long, and weigh 3 to 5 ounces (85 to 142 grams). Dwarf hamsters can range in length from 2 to 4 inches (5.1 to 10.2 centimeters) and weigh ¼₄ to ⅛ ounces (2 to 3 grams).

Hamsters have one of the quickest reproduction rates of any animal. A female hamster carries her young in her body for 16 to 20 days. Newborn hamsters are fully developed by two months of age. However, hamsters do not live a very long time. Depending on the breed or species, hamsters can live between 2 and 3 years. With proper care, some hamsters may live even longer.

14

A hamster and its companion

What Kind of Personality Might a Hamster Have?

Just like human beings, individual hamsters can have their own unique personalities. But certain breeds do tend to have common traits. For example, golden hamsters, whose ancestors lived alone, do not like to live with other hamsters. However, they tend to bond easily with their human family members.

Dwarf hamsters once lived together in the wild, so they like to have the company of their own kind. If you are considering a dwarf hamster as a pet, find a pair—ideally two males or two females from the same litter—that have already bonded.

In general, hamsters that have lived around people and that have been tamed at an early age tend to be more comfortable with human contact. Hamsters must feel safe and secure in their environment. When they do, they are energetic, curious, and playful. They love attention from their owners and enjoy exploring the world around them.

A hamster with full
cheek pouches

What Should You Look for When Choosing a Hamster?

Hamsters should be lively and exhibit a sense of curiosity about their environment. Choose a hamster that has clear, bright eyes. A healthy hamster should also have a clean, even coat of hair, with no thinning or bald patches. Its body should be barrel-shaped and well proportioned—not too thin.

Make sure your hamster's teeth are even, well formed, and well trimmed. Avoid any hamster with teeth that are crooked or out of place. That animal may have trouble eating, which could lead to serious health problems.

Also, take a look at the hamster's nose and rear end. Both should be dry. Dampness or wetness in either of these areas could be a sign of illness.

Young hamsters should be between four and eight weeks old to become a pet.

A healthy hamster

What Does a Hamster Eat?

Hamsters are omnivores *(OM nuh vawrs)*, which means they can eat a little bit of everything. The easiest way to meet your hamster's nutritional needs is with a diet that combines a high-quality dry hamster food (such as hamster pellets) with fresh foods from your own kitchen.

Hamsters need food and water throughout the day. Feeding your hamster a small serving of fresh food every day is a great way to supplement its diet and maintain its interest in eating. Dried vegetables, cooked oats and barley, sunflower seeds, and dog biscuits are all good choices. Small chunks of hard boiled egg or cooked meat can also be given to your hamster.

Hamsters also love treats! Chopped fresh carrots and apples or plain popcorn are excellent treats that you can give to your hamster two or three times a week. Make sure that everything you feed your hamster is fresh and the same quality as what you would eat yourself.

20

A hamster eating

Where Should a Pet Hamster Be Kept?

Hamsters should be kept indoors in a wire cage or a glass or plastic aquarium-style home. When choosing the best home for your hamster, consider the size of the animal and the number of pets. For example, are you housing a single golden hamster, or a pair of dwarfs? Because of their small size, dwarf hamsters may be able to squeeze through the bars of a wire cage, so an aquarium-style home may work best. In addition, dwarfs usually need more space than goldens because they are housed in pairs and tend to be more active.

Any style of housing that you choose for your hamster should be well-ventilated (get lots of fresh air) and easy to clean, have a secure cover, and have at least 19 square inches (122.6 square centimeters) of floor space. A water bottle and food dish are musts.

A hamster cage

How Should You Set Up a Hamster's Cage?

Hamsters are very organized animals. To help keep your hamster happy, create areas in your hamster's home for eating, sleeping, and using the bathroom. Place a few safe toys and a tube or small box in the cage where the hamster can hide or rest. Be sure to keep a 3-inch (7.6-centimeter) layer of clean bedding on the floor of the cage at all times. Choose bedding material that is made from wood shavings (except cedar and pine) topped with shredded paper. Hay and straw or fluffy materials are not recommended.

Place your hamster's cage in a section of your house that is quiet and out of the reach of other household pets. The ideal temperature for a hamster is anywhere from 65 to 80 °F (18 to 27 °C). Keep your hamster's home out of direct sunlight and away from drafts.

Hamsters love places to hide.

25

How Often Should You Clean a Hamster's Cage?

Hamster owners need to remove uneaten food and replace soiled bedding in their hamster's cage once a day. Food dishes and water bottles should also be cleaned every day with warm, soapy water. They should be dried completely before you refill them with fresh food and water.

Your hamster's cage should be thoroughly cleaned once a week. To do this, take the hamster out of the cage and place it in a secure holding cage or container. Next, wash the entire cage and all components, such as tunnels and toys, with mild soapy water. Dry everything before laying out fresh bedding and putting the hamster back inside the cage.

Be sure to wash your hands thoroughly after cleaning your hamster's cage.

Wear gloves when cleaning
a hamster's cage.

27

Should You Groom a Hamster?

Hamsters are experts at grooming themselves, so it is not necessary for you to groom your hamster. However, you may help keep your hamster clean by gently petting or rubbing off any pieces of dirt that you see trapped in its fur.

You may also brush your hamster's coat with a soft toothbrush on occasion, especially if it is the longhaired type. These brushing sessions will also give you the opportunity to inspect your hamster for any physical changes that could indicate illness or injury, such as a lump on its belly or dampness around its rear end.

It is unnecessary to clip a hamster's toenails.

Some hamsters love
to be groomed.

29

Should You Give a Hamster a Bath?

Bathing your hamster is not recommended. Hamsters can go into shock from the change in temperature when they are wet. Getting water in their ears can also cause a deadly infection.

If your hamster has become so dirty that you absolutely must bathe it, use a wet towel to wipe the hamster. A shallow dish filled with 1 to 2 inches (2.5 to 5.1 centimeters) of lukewarm water can also be used. Use a very small amount of mild baby shampoo and wipe your hamster gently. Rinse the hamster and dry it with a towel. Then dry it further with a hair dryer set at its lowest temperature. Be sure to hold it several inches or centimeters away from the hamster. The hamster should be completely dry before you return it to the cage.

Another alternative is to give your hamster a sand bath. Get some chinchilla sand at the pet store. (Make sure it's sand, not dust, which can cause breathing problems in your hamster.) Put the sand in a little bowl for your hamster to roll around in.

A hamster sand bath

31

What Kinds of Exercise or Play Are Needed?

Today's pet hamsters are related to wild hamsters that often had to roam for miles or kilometers in search of food. As a result, hamsters have much energy and need plenty of exercise. Hamsters should have a variety of toys and other objects available to keep them active within their habitats. Rotate the toys that you place within the cage to keep your hamster surprised and interested.

Many hamsters also enjoy exploring the world outside of their cages. Before taking your hamster out of its cage, be sure to enclose the area where the hamster will be. All doors and windows should be closed. Any heating vents or other openings within reach of the hamster should be covered. Electrical cords should also be kept out of reach. Chewing these cords could be deadly to your hamster.

You can set up safe places in your home for your hamster to play.

33

How Do You Help a Hamster Care for Its Young?

Female hamsters with young must have plenty of food and water, along with lots of bedding materials so that they can make a nest. The nest should not be disturbed, and the cage should not be cleaned during this period. Hamsters usually give birth to litters of 6 to 9 puppies (baby hamsters). Newborn pups should not be handled until they are at least 10 days old.

Young hamsters will get most of their food needs from their mother's milk until they are about two weeks old. Then you can gradually introduce the same foods that their mother eats, giving them hamster pellets soaked in water at first. Be sure to have plenty of water available, too.

When the pups are between 7 and 8 weeks old, you should separate males and females to prevent further breeding. Try to place these young hamsters in loving homes if you are unable to care for them yourself.

A mother hamster
and her pups

35

What Are Some Other Kinds of Rodents?

Almost half of all mammalian species (species that are mammals) are rodents. Many of the small mammals that you see outside are rodents, including squirrels, beavers, and gophers. Some rodents have had almost no contact with human beings, while others have been bred and raised by people as beloved pets.

Some of the most popular pet rodents are gerbils *(JUR buhls)*, mice, rats, guinea *(GIHN ee)* pigs, and chinchillas. You will read about these rodents on the following pages.

Most pet rodents are relatively easy to care for, which makes them popular pets for families with young children. However, it is not a good idea to capture a wild rodent and make it a pet. The animal may carry harmful diseases and is not likely to be tameable.

A beaver

What Is a Gerbil?

A gerbil is a small, furry rodent with long hind legs and a long, hairy tail. There are many different kinds of gerbils, but the one most commonly kept as a pet is the Mongolian gerbil. These gerbils come in a variety of colors and have a body length of about 8 inches (20 centimeters), including the tail. Though gerbils generally walk on four legs, they occasionally hop like kangaroos on their hind legs.

Gerbils are social animals and should be kept as pairs (either two males or two females) or as families. Gerbils tend to be affectionate, so you may observe them cuddling or sleeping together or grooming each other. They can also be quite playful and may wrestle or chase each other around the cage. But some gerbils don't get along well and should be separated if these "play dates" turn into actual fights.

Gerbils are omnivores, but their primary diet should be made up of food pellets for pet mice or rats, fruit, seeds, and raw vegetables. They live an average of four years.

Gerbils

39

What Is a Mouse?

Mice are small rodents that often live near human beings, building nests in their homes and eating their food. Some people do everything they can to keep mice out of their homes, but many people keep them as pets!

The most common kind of pet mouse is the house mouse. These mice can come in a variety of colors, from grayish-brown to white. A domestic mouse usually measures from 2½ to 3½ inches (6 to 9 centimeters) long without the tail. The tail grows about the same length as the body. Most house mice weigh ½ to 1 ounce (14 to 28 grams).

One drawback to having pet mice is that they are active mainly at night, so your mice will likely be inactive during the day. Mice are happier when living in pairs or small groups. Unless you plan to breed your mice, a group of females is the best choice.

As with other small rodents, pet mice usually have fairly short lives. On average, they live for only about two years.

What Is a Rat?

A rat is a furry, long-tailed rodent that looks a bit like a large mouse. Most people think of rats as disease-spreading pests, but tame rats can make safe, gentle pets. Rats are intelligent and curious, so they can be fun to watch.

The best-known species of rat are the black rat and the brown rat. Black rats can grow between 7 to 8 inches (18 to 20 centimeters) long, not including their tail, and weigh about 10 ounces (280 grams). Brown rats measure from 8 to 10 inches (20 to 25 centimeters) long, not including their tail, and weigh up to 16 ounces (485 grams). The most common pet rat is the white rat, which is a variety of the brown rat.

Like mice, rats are active mainly at night. They are also social animals that like to live in pairs or groups. It is best to separate males from females if you do keep more than one rat.

Rats tend to need more attention than other pet rodents, but the companionship they offer can be very rewarding.

A pet rat

What Is a Guinea Pig?

Guinea pigs are medium-sized rodents with shiny eyes and plump, furry bodies. They are smaller than a cat but larger than a mouse. A full-sized guinea pig can be anywhere from about 10 to 14 inches (25 to 36 centimeters) long and weigh between 2 and 3 pounds (0.9 and 1.4 kilograms).

There are many different breeds of guinea pig. They come in a variety of colors, including black, brown, red, white, or a combination of colors. Some have been bred to have short or long, straight hair, while others have silky, curly hair. Guinea pigs with long hair need to be groomed more than other pet rodents—usually several times a week.

Guinea pigs can make great pets because they are often cuddly and sweet-tempered. Most guinea pigs enjoy attention and are relatively easy to care for. A guinea pig can live 7 or 8 years, or longer.

Guinea pigs

What Is a Chinchilla?

Chinchillas are rodents with long, thick, gray fur and a bushy tail. There are two types of chinchillas: the long-tailed chinchilla and short-tailed chinchilla. Chinchillas have chunky bodies that measure about 11 to 18 inches (28 to 46 centimeters) long, including the tail. Females grow larger than males.

Wild chinchillas live in the Andes Mountains in South America. Their heavy fur helps to keep them warm in this cold, rocky environment. Long, strong hind limbs allow them to run and jump easily on rocky surfaces. The animals come out at night to search for such food as grasses, bulbs, and roots. Pet chinchillas are also active at night.

For a long time, people have used the chinchilla's soft fur to make luxurious coats. Because they have been hunted for their valuable fur, wild chinchillas are extremely rare in their natural habitats.

Chinchillas are gentle, clean, and quiet pets. Like many other pet rodents, they are playful and need daily exercise. They are usually easy to tame, though some do not like to be held.

A long-tailed chinchilla

47

How Should You Pick Up a Hamster?

Hamsters explore the world using their sense of smell and their hearing. Allow your hamster to get familiar with your voice and your scent during your first few days together before you try to pick it up. Speak softly to your hamster while you are feeding it or cleaning its bedding. Always approach it from the front, never from above or behind.

Before you try to pick up your hamster, place your hand inside the cage. Allow the hamster to sniff your skin and get accustomed to your scent. Repeat these taming exercises until the hamster readily approaches you or hops into your hand. This may take days, or even weeks.

Once your hamster is ready to be handled, gently scoop up the hamster with one hand cupped to hold it underneath the front of its body, and the other cupped under its rear end. If your hamster is asleep, it is best not to wake it to hold it. Also, if your hamster bares its teeth or snaps at you, it likely does not want to be held at that time.

Be gentle when holding
your hamster.

What Kinds of Fun Can You Have with Your Hamster?

You should take your hamster out of the cage every day and allow it to explore a small area in your house. Use empty cardboard toilet paper or paper towel rolls to set up mazes for your hamster. Piping and tubing systems available from the pet store are also fun for your hamster.

Be aware that your hamster will gnaw through anything that is made out of cardboard and other soft materials, so change these items frequently. Hamsters can also gnaw through plastic, so check your hamster's toys regularly to make sure they are in good condition. Discard anything with sharp or pointed edges, as these could harm your hamster.

When your hamster is roaming outside of its cage, make sure other household pets are safely confined in another room, and alert other family members that the hamster will be out of the cage. Keep a close watch on your hamster when it is out and about, and be mindful of where you step as you move around the room with your pet.

Hamsters love to climb and explore.

What Kinds of Toys Should Hamsters Play With?

A wheel is one of the most popular toys for hamsters. Wheels are fun for hamsters to run on and also give the animal needed exercise. The safest kind is solid, with no open spaces. Rotate the wheel with other toys so the hamster doesn't become bored. Plastic hamster balls that come in a variety of sizes are a good option.

You can make your own toys using simple objects like cardboard tubes that hamsters can crawl through. Try also giving your hamster untreated wooden spools or blocks to chew on and climb over in its cage. These will also help the animal to keep its teeth well trimmed. (See page 54.)

Make sure that all of your hamster's toys are made from nontoxic materials, and that they are free from sharp edges or small pieces that could break off and be swallowed or cause injury to your hamster's cheek pouches.

A hamster on a wheel

Can a Hamster's Teeth Get Too Long?

A hamster's teeth continue to grow for its entire life. You can help your hamster keep its teeth healthy and at the right length by giving it things to gnaw on.

If a hamster's teeth grow too long, the animal will not be able to eat and can get sick. Long teeth can also injure the animal's mouth and face. To help a hamster keep its teeth the right length, give it untreated wooden spools or blocks and foods like hamster pellets, dog biscuits, and crunchy fresh vegetables that will help to wear its teeth down.

If your hamster is unable to eat or is losing weight, there may be something wrong with its teeth. Ask your veterinarian to check. A vet should trim teeth that are seriously overgrown.

A hamster gnawing on a branch

What Are Some Common Signs of Illness?

Animals cannot tell people if they are sick or hurt, so you must observe your hamster's behavior for changes. If your pet is less active than usual or irritable, or does not seem interested in food or water, it may be ill. Another sign of illness is constant scratching, a thin coat, and bare spots.

If your hamster begins sneezing and its eyes are cloudy or tearing, but its behavior hasn't changed, it may have an allergy. To see if food is causing the allergy, feed your hamster only hamster pellets for a while. Then introduce other foods one at a time and observe how it reacts. If that doesn't work, try using a different kind of bedding. Your hamster may be allergic to the bedding material or dust particles. If symptoms remain, call your veterinarian.

If your hamster develops diarrhea, it could mean your pet has an infection. You should call your veterinarian immediately.

Healthy hamsters should have bright, alert eyes.

What Routine Veterinary Care Is Needed?

Hamsters usually do not require much routine care from a veterinarian, but you should take your hamster to the vet's office if it becomes sick or hurt.

You may want to take the hamster to the vet soon after you get it so he or she can make sure your pet is healthy. You can also ask the vet for advice on how to care for your hamster.

Monitor your pet closely and call or take it to the vet if your hamster begins to act differently. See page 56 for common signs of illness in hamsters.

A hamster getting a
medical checkup

What Are Your Responsibilities as an Owner?

Responsibility is a job or task you promise to do. As the owner of a hamster, you are responsible for your pet's health and well-being. You must perform daily chores, such as giving your animal proper food and exercise and keeping its cage clean.

To keep your pet hamster healthy and happy, you must respect its habits and lifestyle. As nocturnal creatures, many hamsters are more active during the evening and night, and need to rest during the day. Try not to disturb your hamster when it is resting.

Also, some hamsters, such as the golden, prefer to live alone. Others, such as the dwarfs, thrive when they are housed in pairs. Learn about your hamster's preferences, and try to accommodate them. This will lead to happier hamsters, and a better relationship with your pet.

Hamsters are lovable companions.

Hamster Fun Facts

→ A hamster can store large amounts of food and bedding materials in its cheek pouches. When full, a hamster's cheek pouches can nearly double the width of its head!

→ Hamsters are excellent escape artists. They have been known to unhook loose latches on their cages, or slip away while outside of their habitats. Lost hamsters have been discovered in drawers and cabinets, and under furniture cushions and even the sheets of an owner's bed!

→ Hamsters have a lot of energy. When they run on a hamster wheel or in a hamster ball, they could generate enough power to run small appliances! People have experimented with small hamster-powered vacuum cleaners, paper shredders, and night lights.

→ Some hamsters are bred for hamster shows. Show hamsters are judged on their size, color, and the quality of their fur.

→ Hamsters are great housekeepers. In the wild, they build burrows with many different tunnels and rooms for eating, sleeping, and taking care of their pups—much like a human home.

Glossary

allergy A reaction, or change, caused by something that would not ordinarily be harmful.

ancestor An animal from which another animal is directly descended. Usually, *ancestor* is used to refer to an animal more removed than a parent or grandparent.

breed To produce animals by carefully selecting and mating them for certain traits. Also, a group of animals having the same type of ancestors.

burrow A hole dug in the ground by an animal for shelter. Also, to dig a hole in the ground.

colony A group of animals or plants of the same kind, living or growing together.

groom To take care of an animal, for example, by combing, brushing, or trimming its coat.

habitat Where an animal lives.

incisor A tooth having a sharp edge for cutting; one of the front teeth in mammals between the canine teeth.

litter The young animals produced by an animal at one birthing.

mammal A type of animal that feeds its young with milk made by the mother.

nocturnal Active at night.

omnivore An animal that eats both animals and plants.

puppy A young hamster.

rodent A type of mammal having two continually growing incisor teeth used for gnawing.

species A group of animals that have certain permanent characteristics in common and are able to produce offspring.

trait A feature or characteristic particular to an animal or breed of animals.

Index

(**Boldface** indicates a photo, map, or illustration.)

For more information about hamsters and other pet rodents, try these resources:

Books:
Hamsters and Gerbils by Jimmy Johnson (Smart Apple Media, 2009)

Hamsters, Gerbils, Guinea Pigs, Rabbits, Ferrets, Mice, and Rats by Laura S. Jeffrey (Enslow Publishers, 2004)

Is My Hamster Wild? The Secret Lives of Hamsters, Gerbils, and Guinea Pigs by Rain Newcomb and Rose McLarney (Lark Books, 2008)

Silkies and Other Guinea Pigs (World Book, 2007)

The Wild Side of Pet Hamsters by Jo Waters (Raintree, 2005)

Web sites:
Hamsterific
http://www.hamsterific.com

ASPCA (The American Society for the Prevention of Cruelty to Animals)

http://www.aspca.org/pet-care/small-pet-care/

Chinchilla Planet
http://www.chinchillaplanet.com/

Comparing Pet Rodents
http://exoticpets.about.com/cs/resourcesgeneral/a/choosearodent.htm

Hamster Classification

Scientists classify animals by placing them into groups. The animal kingdom is a group that contains all the world's animals. Phylum, class, order, and family are smaller groups. Each phylum contains many classes. A class contains orders, an order contains families, and a family contains genuses. One or more species belong to each genus. Each species has its own scientific name. Here is how the animals in this book fit into this system.

Animals with backbones and their relatives (Phylum Chordata)
Mammals (Class Mammalia)
Rodents (Order Rodentia)

Hamsters, gerbils, mice, rats (Family Muridae)

Chinchilla (Family Chinchilladae)

Guinea pig (Family Caviidae)